TRIBES of NATIVE AMERICA

Pomo

edited by Marla Felkins Ryan
and Linda Schmittroth

BLACKBIRCH®
PRESS

THOMSON
━━━✦━━━ ™
GALE

San Diego • Detroit • New York • San Francisco • Cleveland
New Haven, Conn. • Waterville, Maine • London • Munich

Photo credits: Cover © Library of Congress; cover © National Archives; cover Courtesy of Northwestern University Library; cover © PhotoDisc; cover © Perry Jasper Photography; cover © Picturequest; cover © Seattle Post-Intelligencer Collection, Museum of History & Industry; cover, pages 6-7 © Photospin; pages 5, 10, 16, 21, 24 © Corbis; pages 8, 20 © Hulton Archive; pages 11, 12, 13, 18, 20, 22, 27 © Sun Valley Photography/nativestock.com; pages 14, 26, 28, 29 © Marilyn "Angel" Wynn/nativestock.com; pages 19, 23, 26 © Corel

LIBRARY OF CONGRESS CATALOGING-IN-PUBLICATION DATA

Pomo / Marla Felkins Ryan, book editor ; Linda Schmittroth, book editor.
   v. cm. — (Tribes of Native America)
Includes bibliographical references and index.
Contents: Name — Origins and group affiliations — The Navajo code talkers — Economy — Daily life — Education — Healing practices — Customs — Current tribal issues.
 ISBN 1-56711-629-9 (alk. paper)
  1. Pomo Indians—Juvenile literature. [1. Pomo Indians. 2. Indians of North America— California.] I. Ryan, Marla Felkins. II. Schmittroth, Linda. III. Series.
  E99.P65 P65 2003
  979.4004'9757—dc21
                                                                        2002008671

Printed in United States
10 9 8 7 6 5 4 3 2 1

Table of Contents

• FIRST LOOK •

POMO

Name

Pomo (pronounced *PO-mo*) means "at red earth hole."

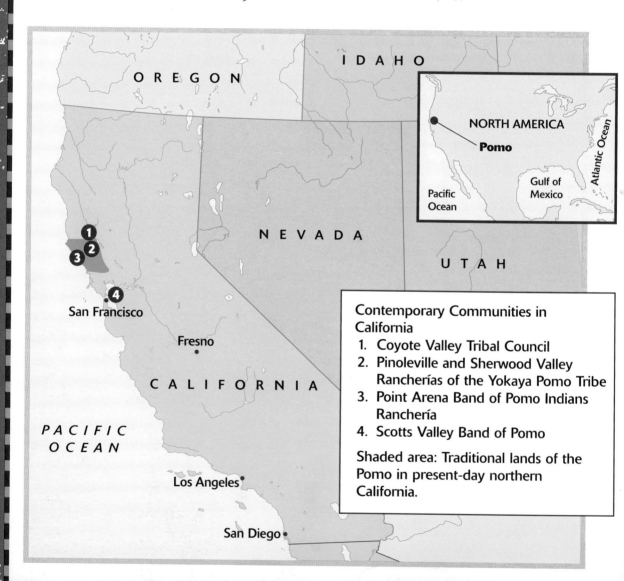

Contemporary Communities in California
1. Coyote Valley Tribal Council
2. Pinoleville and Sherwood Valley Rancherías of the Yokaya Pomo Tribe
3. Point Arena Band of Pomo Indians Ranchería
4. Scotts Valley Band of Pomo

Shaded area: Traditional lands of the Pomo in present-day northern California.

Ray Brown, a Pomo leader, poses in front of buildings constructed in traditional ways.

Where are the traditional Pomo lands?

The Pomo lived in northern California. Their lands were near Clear Lake and the Russian River in present-day Mendocino, Sonoma, and Lake counties. Today, they live on or near about two dozen isolated rancherías (small ranches) and reservations.

What has happened to the population?

In the early 1800s, there were between 13,000 and 20,000 Pomo. In a 1990 population count by the U.S. Bureau of the Census, 4,766 people said they were Pomo.

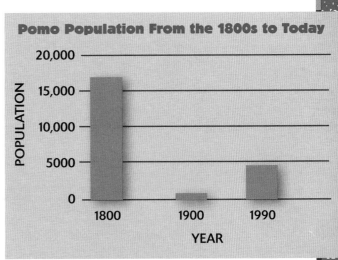

Pomo Population From the 1800s to Today

Origins and group ties

The Pomo lived in the hills and valleys north of present-day San Francisco for more than 10,000 years. There were more than 70 Pomo tribes. They were part of seven groups. These groups were the Northern Pomo, Central Pomo, Southern Pomo, Southwestern Pomo or Kashaya, Eastern Pomo, Southeastern Pomo, and Northeastern Pomo.

Marin County (now connected to San Francisco by the Golden Gate Bridge) was once Pomo land.

For thousands of years, the Pomo lived calm, orderly lives filled with laughter and song. After they met Europeans, their story became a tragic one. Russians, Spaniards, Mexicans, and Americans killed them, polluted their lands, and made them slaves. By the late 19th century, there were only about 1,000 Pomo. They were homeless. The Pomo won back some land in the twentieth century, and their population began to grow.

HISTORY

Russians in Pomo lands

Little is known about Pomo history and ways of life before they met Europeans in the nineteenth century. Groups of Pomo lived over a large area, so they did not always meet people from the same nations. Each group of Europeans—Russians, Spanish, Mexicans, and Americans—played a part in the near-destruction of this large California tribe.

The Kashaya Pomo lived along the Pacific coast in what is now northwest Sonoma County. They were the only Pomo who had contact with Russians, who set up Fort Ross in 1811 on Bodega

The Kashaya Pomo encountered Russian fur traders who built Fort Ross in 1811.

Bay. The Russians were there to make profits from sea otter furs. They treated the Pomo cruelly. They kidnapped and enslaved Pomo women and children. These victims were held hostage to force Pomo men to hand over furs and food.

The Pomo fought back with a few escapes and small-scale attacks. By the time the Russians left in 1842, many of the Kashaya Pomo had died from murder, overwork, or diseases brought by whites.

Spanish, Mexicans, and the Southern Pomo

Meanwhile, the Spanish, who claimed to own California, feared that the Russians or British would take it over. They set up forts and missions to protect California for Spanish settlement. The missions would convert natives to the Roman Catholic religion. They would also teach them skills so they could become slaves or workers for the Spanish.

In 1822, California became part of the Mexican Republic, and the missions were closed. Mexicans took over Pomo lands. This led to fights, especially in the Clear Lake region. Between 1834 and 1847, Mexican soldiers captured or killed thousands of Pomo. Slavery and epidemics of smallpox and cholera killed thousands more.

1817
The first Spanish mission is founded in Pomo land

1850
U.S. army kills most residents of a small Pomo village

1856
Many Pomo move to the Mendocino and Round Valley

1861
American Civil War begins

1881
Pomo chiefs start a fund-raising drive to buy rancherías

1958
The state of California ends the status of many Indian tribes, including the Pomo rancherías

1980
Pomo woman Tillie Hardwick begins a fight for federal recognition of rancherías. In 1983, she wins her case, and reservation status is restored to 17 California rancherías

1990s
The fight for federal recognition of all Pomo rancherías goes on

The Spanish built missions like this one along the California coast.

Americans mistreat the Pomo

The United States won California from Mexico in 1848. It became a state in 1850. American settlers poured in and began to seize native lands. Relations were hostile between these new settlers and the Pomo.

Matters came to a head after white landowners Andrew Kelsey and Charles Stone were killed. The pair had forced hundreds of Pomo to work on their ranch. The Pomo were tired of being starved, beaten, and shot. Some of them rebelled. They killed both white men, then fled to the hills.

American soldiers were sent to catch the Pomo who had killed Kelsey and Stone. When they found a peaceful group of Eastern Pomo on a small island on Clear Lake, they slaughtered the innocent men, women, and children. The soldiers then went eastward. They killed any Pomo they met along the way.

The Pomo rebelled against whites in 1850.

Move to reservations

The government hoped to end the violence in California. In 1851, it sent agents to make treaties with the Indian tribes. California tribes, including the Pomo, agreed to give up most of their lands. In exchange, they would get about 7.5 million acres to be set aside as reservations.

White Californians were horrified that the Indians were to receive so much land. The area was about 8 percent of the state. They were also afraid that the Indians who had been their slaves would move to reservations. They protested so much that the U.S. Senate rejected the treaties. Soon after, a much smaller area of 1.2 million acres was set aside for reservations.

The Pomo were forced to move to the Mendocino and Round Valley reservations. Their lands were taken over by white settlers. In 1867, the Mendocino Reservation was closed. Many of the Pomo were left without homes. Some went back to their old lands. There, they found that whites had taken the best land. The Pomo settled on some poor, unwanted pieces. Their numbers declined as many died from diseases. At the same time, their customs and beliefs began to disappear.

A Pomo fishing camp

The Pomo relied on fishing for survival.

By the turn of the twentieth century, there were just over 1,000 Pomo. They lived in poverty. They survived on fish, game, plants, and the few items they could afford to buy. The whites saw them as second-class citizens and discriminated against them.

Landowners again

Native groups later began to recover. They united to buy pieces of their old lands. Pomo groups pooled the small sums they earned in their work on white-owned ranches and from sales of their beautiful feathered baskets. They bought the rancherías (small ranches) of Pinoleville and Yokaya.

The Pomo earned money by selling handmade baskets.

Religious groups and some government officials got involved in the rancheria movement. The Indian Reorganization Act of 1934 was partly designed to stop the damage done by previous Indian policies. It supplied money to buy more reservations and rancherías. The Pomo bought more land. They also learned how to use the American justice system to their advantage. In 1907, an Eastern Pomo named Ethan Anderson filed a lawsuit. It helped Indian groups win the right to vote. Native Americans were granted full U.S. citizenship in 1924.

New policies

New government policies in the 1950s changed the status of California rancherías. The rancherías agreed to give up their federal recognition (a status that gives special benefits and financial aid). In return, the Bureau of Indian Affairs promised to help improve life on the rancherías. This promise was not kept. Instead, Pomo land was divided among members of the rancherías. Many of the owners later lost their land when they could not make mortgage or tax payments.

By the 1970s, it was clear to the Pomo that the Bureau of Indian Affairs was not going help them make improvements on the former rancherías. A Pomo woman named Tillie Hardwick filed a lawsuit against the United States. She won, and several rancherías got back their federal recognition.

Today, the Pomo work to keep their culture, language, and arts alive. At the same time, they look for ways to expand their land. They also earn money from the tourists who flock to see their beautiful homeland.

Religion

The Pomo believed in many spirits. Among them was a creator-hero who gave his name to a secret religious society called Kuksu. The Kuksu Society was open only to a small group of men. They were

the beauty of Pomo lands has helped make tourism a source of income for the tribe.

selected while very young to go through a long training process. Once they became members, they carried out many of the village's ceremonies and public affairs. At ceremonies, Kuksu dancers pretended to be spirits. They wore special

headpieces made of sticks with feathers at the ends. Their bodies were painted black. The rituals brought good harvests or protection against disaster or attack.

A religious group called the Ghost Society was open to all young men. In some Pomo groups, women could join, too. The Ghost Society did dances to honor the dead. Both the Ghost and the Kuksu societies were led by professional spiritual guides, or shamans (pronounced SHAH-munz or SHAY-munz).

Ghost dances and dream dances

After the move to reservations, the Pomo adopted the Ghost Dance religion of 1870. It was supposed to rid the world of white people. When it failed to do so, the Bole-Maru, or New Ghost Dance, religion was adopted.

Bole-Maru translates roughly as "spirits of the dead." It used parts of the old Ghost Society and the Ghost Dance religion. Its leaders were people who had visions in dreams. Some visions included songs and dances, which were taught to the tribe. The religion stressed moral behavior. It also had a belief in an afterlife and a supreme being. It forbade people to drink, fight, and steal. Many Pomo still practice the Bole-Maru religion today.

A Pomo village, around 1875.

Government

At one time, there were more than 70 Pomo tribes. They were divided into groups called tribelets. These ranged in size from 125 to more than 500 persons. In a tribelet, one main village was surrounded by a few outlying settlements. Villages were made up of one or more family groups. Villages chose a family group to be their leaders. Some villages had only one chief. Others had as many as 20. Today, most Pomo reservations and rancherías are run by elected tribal councils.

Economy

The Pomo mainly hunted and gathered. They also traded with money, though. Pomo money came in two forms. One was clamshells, which were ground into circles. Each had a hole bored into it, and was strung on strings. Beads made from a mineral called magnesite (pronounced MAG-nuh-site) were also used as money. When magnesite was treated with fire, it turned different shades of pink, orange, and tan.

The Pomo made money out of clamshells.

The value of clamshell disks depended on their age, thickness, and the length of the strung disks. Magnesite beads were more valuable. They were traded individually rather than strung.

Because they used money, the Pomo won a reputation as great counters. They could deal in sums in the tens of thousands without the use of multiplication or division. Their knowledge of money was useful when they wanted to buy land from the government.

After the reservations

Pomo rancherías were always too small to support many people. By the late 19th century, the people had to seek work on white-owned lands. They

Pomo women made and sold baskets to earn money.

picked fruit and hops (a plant used to make beer). Women wove baskets to sell or did other people's laundry. Meanwhile, the traditional ways of hunting and gathering were all but lost.

Both World War I (1914-1918) and World War II (1939-1945) brought jobs for Pomo men. Many went to serve in the military or took jobs in cities. Women went to work as maids. Today, only about one-third of the Pomo live on rancherías and reservations. They still struggle to support themselves.

Pomo men were among the Native Americans who fought in World War II.

DAILY LIFE

Families

The family has always been very important to the Pomo. Traditionally, they shared land and homes with family members in close-knit communities.

Buildings

Three types of structures were common to all Pomo groups. These were dwelling houses, temporary or seasonal shelters, and sweathouses or ceremonial houses built partly underground. Building materials and shapes varied.

In redwood land, family homes were often cone-shaped houses made of slabs of redwood bark. These were only 8 to 15 feet in diameter and perhaps 6 feet in height. Though most were single-family homes, they sometimes housed as many as 12 people. Assembly or ceremonial houses could be much larger. Some were as big as 70 feet in diameter. They were

Some Pomo buildings, like this one, were dome-shaped.

THE HIGH STATUS OF WOMEN

Unlike most Native American women, Pomo women enjoyed a fairly high status. They could be chiefs. Some became part of the tribe's secret societies. They were barred from some other societies, however. Some of these societies even held performances meant to frighten women.

A Pomo woman gathers seeds.

Young couples often lived with the bride's family in homes occupied by several families. The oldest wife in the house was its owner. In modern times, many skilled Pomo women wove beautiful baskets that were sold to support the tribe. Their earnings helped buy back land for the Pomo after they lost their lands.

held up by beams and partially covered with earth. From a distance, they looked like tiny hills.

Valley and lake Pomo tended to build circular, rectangular, or L-shaped structures of brush or reeds. Clear Lake groups used a plant material called tule (pronounced TOO-lee) to build homes up to 40 feet in length that could hold 20 people. These homes could house several families.

The Pomo hunted large animals such as deer.

Food

All Pomo groups had abundant natural resources. They knew the best times to hunt and gather certain foods.

Fish were caught with spears, basketry traps, or nets by fishermen in lightweight, raft-like canoes. Deer, elk, and antelope were hunted. The Pomo hunted with bows and arrows, spears, and even clubs. Some birds were hunted. Others, however, such as the crow and owl, were not. They were too important in the Pomo religion.

Insects, such as grasshoppers and caterpillars, were gathered and eaten. Grasses, roots, berries, nuts, bulbs, and edible greens were eaten while in

Acorns were a food source for the Pomo.

season. The favorite vegetable food was the acorn. Ground acorn meal was eaten daily. It was generally served as a mush, along with dried blackfish.

Education

Older Pomo men and women were well respected. They spent a great deal of time with the young. Special bonds formed between elders and youngsters. In some groups, a young boy might sleep with his grandfather. He kept the old man warm at night. In return, the grandfather taught him tribal history.

After they moved to reservations, Pomo children faced many hardships. Nearby towns would not let them go to public schools. Pomo parents filed lawsuits to challenge this practice. In one instance, the local school board set up a separate school for Indian children. In 1923, a Pomo man filed a lawsuit that ended school segregation (separation by race or class) in Mendocino County.

Clothing

Pomo men rarely wore clothing. Sometimes, though, they put on a breechcloth, a garment with front and back flaps that hung from the waist. Women wore long skirts of shredded bark or tule. Both sexes sometimes wore mantles, cape-like garments made of hide or woven plant fibers that tied at the neck and were belted at the waist. Wealthy people kept warm with blankets made of rabbit hides or other skins. The poor made do with shredded willow bark or other fiber. The Pomo usually went barefoot. For special occasions, they might wear deer-hide boots and tule moccasins.

Both sexes kept their hair long. Women wore ear ornaments decorated with beads and feathers. Clamshell beads, abalone shells, and feathers were used in belts, neckbands, and wristbands. Some women wore dance headdresses made of fur, feathers, and beads.

Healing practices

Pomo healing was closely tied to religion. Shamans set broken bones. They also treated ailments, such as stomach problems, with herbs. Pomo believed most illnesses came about because the patient did something to anger the spirits or another member of the group. Shamans sang or sucked out the poison that caused the sickness. There were also bear doctors, who paid an annual fee for their position. They wore a bear's skin and head. These were thought to have the power both to heal and cause illness.

Pomo baskets were sometimes decorated with shells or beads.

Arts

The Pomo were known for the baskets they wove from a large variety of roots and other fibers, as well as shells and feathers. Pomo basketry and other crafts have been kept alive by internationally known basket weavers. Among them are Elsie Allen, Mabel McKay, and Laura Fish Somersol.

Oral literature

Coyote the trickster played a big role in Pomo literature. Coyote brought the sun to the Pomo and did other favors. He could also get angry, though. Pomo stories tell how Coyote flooded the world to punish people who were cruel to his children.

The coyote was a character in many traditional Pomo stories.

CUSTOMS

Festivals and ceremonies

Songs and dances have always been an important part of Pomo ceremonies. That tradition continues today. Some rancherías have even built dance houses. The Pinoleville Band of Pomo Indians began to host a yearly Big Time Cultural Awareness Gathering in 1994. It gives the Pomo people a chance to reunite and take part in traditional songs and dances. The Big Time is open to the public.

Pomo dancers

Courtship and marriage

Parents arranged marriages. Children did not have to take the suitors their parents picked for them, but they could not marry someone else without their parents' approval. In many Pomo groups, there was a trial period in which a couple lived together in the woman's home before gifts were exchanged and the marriage

The Pomo used woven cradles like this one.

took place. Some couples stayed with the groom's or bride's parents until they had children. Then, a new door would be cut in the home for them and a new fire and sleeping area added. Young couples did not generally move out on their own.

Childbirth

A woman normally gave birth in her family's home. Afterward, she was given gifts by both sides of the family. The gifts were usually long ropes of clamshell beads. Among the Eastern Pomo, the father could not leave his home for up to eight days after the birth. He was not allowed to hunt, gamble, or dance for a month. Children had two names. One was chosen by the mother's brother and one by the father's brother. Children were often named after deceased relatives.

Puberty

Special ceremonies were performed for boys and girls when they reached puberty. Eastern Pomo girls were purified in a steam ceremony. In it, the girl lay on a tule mat with hot coals all around. On the fourth night, she bathed and received a basket of acorns. She used a complex process to make acorn mush, then served it to her family.

Throughout their youth, boys were given songs to learn. At age 12, they received a bow and a fancy beaded hair net. A few boys were chosen each year to train to become members of the Kuksu Society.

As part of a special ceremony, Pomo girls ground acorns to make mush.

Death and funerals

After a death, the body lay in the house for four days so that its spirit could leave. Mourning was public and dramatic. Female relatives cried and scratched themselves deeply enough to leave scars. Hair was cut short and gifts were brought. The body was then taken outside and burned, face down and pointing to the south. The home and its contents were often burned, too.

Current tribal issues

A major issue for the Pomo is federal recognition of rancherías. The largest Pomo settlement, Hopland Ranchería, is among those that still seek recognition. Other important issues are the struggle to buy more land and to provide housing for tribal members.

Since the 1970s, the Pomo have fought attempts by businesses to build on sacred grounds. The waters of Clear Lake have been polluted by wastes from abandoned mines, by homes and resorts built around it, and by boats that race on it.

Notable people

Elsie Allen (1899-1990) was a well-known Pomo basket weaver, scholar, educator, cultural preservationist, and writer. She kept the art of basket weaving alive and created a worldwide interest in it.

Mabel McKay (1907-1993) was a Pomo-Wintu-Patwin basket weaver, doctor, and cultural preservationist.

Pomo elder, chief, and tribal historian William Benson (1860-1930) was one of the few Pomo men who made baskets. He turned to this craft when there was no longer a need for the fish traps that Pomo men usually made.

For More Information

Giese, Paula. *The California Pomo People, Brief History.* History of the Pomo people of California, written by Paula Giese of the Native American Books Web site. http://indy4.fdl.cc.mn.us~isk/art/basket/pomohist.html

McAuliffe, Claudeen E. "Elsie Allen," in *Notable Native Americans.* Sharon Malinowski, ed. Detroit: Gale, 1995.

Poole, William. *Return of the Sinkyone.* Sierra. 81 (November/December 1996): 52–55, 72.

Glossary

Discriminate to treat someone differently based on religion, class, or race

Pollute to poison

Rancherías small ranches

Reservation plot of land set aside by the United States government for Native Americans

Slaves people forced to work for others, often not for pay

Treaty agreement

Tribe a group of people who live together in a community

Index